GRAND TETON
NATIONAL PARK
WHERE LIGHTNING WALKS

PHOTOGRAPHS BY PAT O'HARA, TEXT BY TIM MCNULTY
DESIGN BY MCQUISTON & DAUGHTER

PUBLISHED BY WOODLANDS PRESS, DEL MAR, CALIFORNIA IN CONJUNCTION WITH GRAND TETON NATURAL HISTORY ASSOCIATION

SNAKE RIVER AND TETON PEAKS
OPPOSITE PAGE: BALD EAGLE, PHOTO BY TOM MANGELSEN

CONTENTS

Introduction—The Drama of Seasons . . . 7
The Mountains—Where Lightning Walks . . . 17
The Valley—In the Lee of the Range . . . 43
Acknowledgments and Photographic Notes . . . 72

ALASKA BASIN
OPPOSITE PAGE: PORCUPINE, PHOTO BY JEFF FOOTT

INTRODUCTION

THE DRAMA OF SEASONS

On the S. W. stands the 3 Tetons whose hard frightful forms rising abruptly from the Lake and towering above the clouds casts a gloomy shade upon the waters beneath whilst the water rushes in torrents down the awful precipices from the snow by which they are crowned . . .

Thus did the early trapper and explorer Osborne Russell describe the Tetons from his camp on the shore of Jackson Lake. Russell was one of the few trappers who left a record of his impressions. For Russell, the grand wall of pinnacles, rock ribs, snowy ridges, and thunderous canyons that formed the Teton Range was a frightful and foreboding obstacle. The snowed-in passes of the range were a hindrance to many trappers on their way to and from the profitable trapping grounds, and though many features now bear names from the trapping period, neither the high range of mountains nor the broad valley called Jackson Hole at its feet was a place the trappers spent much time. Their way was to take from one place and move on to the next. When beaver populations dwindled—as they quickly did—the trappers were soon gone. They were not the first humans to visit the area that was to become Grand Teton National Park, nor would their way of life or relationship to the land endure for more than a generation.

Glaciers choked the mountain canyons, and glacial ice may still have lingered in Jackson Lake, when paleo-Indian peoples first came to Jackson Hole. From as far back as possibly 12,000 years ago, the People made their annual trek through mountain passes to summer encampments beneath the towering peaks of the Tetons. Their long summer days were filled with the gathering of plant foods and the occasional hunting of whatever game was available. Root bulbs of the blue camas were carefully roasted among grasses and herbs. Bitterroot, sego lilies, and berries were gathered and dried.

The passage from paleolithic summer dwelling place to national park was by no means a smooth one. Although Ferdinand V. Hayden visited the Tetons in 1860 and again in the 1870s, the Teton Range and Jackson Hole were not among his recommendations for a national park in the region. Consequently, when Yellowstone, our country's first national park, was created in 1872, it included none of the scenic Teton country to the south. Later attempts by Congress to include the Tetons were thwarted. It wasn't until 1897, with the establishment of a Teton Forest Reserve, that the area was set aside. 1929 saw the creation of Grand Teton National Park, but the original park was small, confined to the steep mountainous country and the small lakes at the feet of its canyons, and no protection was given to the important wildlife range of the valley of Jackson Hole. However, by 1950 a compromise bill was passed that expanded the park to include much of the area of Jackson Hole, Jackson Lake, and the rich corridor of the Snake River.

Today Grand Teton National Park encompasses 310,516 acres of sagebrush flats, rivers, forests, morainal lakes, and steep, rugged peaks and canyons. Protected are wildlife habitats and vegetation zones that range from about 6500 feet in the valley to 13,770 feet at the summit of the Grand Teton.

The nearly flat floor of Jackson Hole lies in sharp contrast to the precipitous rise of the east flank of the Teton Range. The spectacular mountain uplift and subsequent shaping by the erosive powers of wind, water, and glaciers have created what is perhaps the most dramatic and classically beautiful mountainscape in North America. The eastern escarpment of the range is the leading edge of an uplifted fault block. The fault zone along which it rose runs north and south along the eastern base of the range. Exposed along this face is some of the oldest bedrock on the continent. Throughout the

9 million years of its sporadic uplift, the mountain wall has been assailed by the erosive powers of wind, water, frost action, and most recently, glaciers. It was the quarrying power of glaciers that sculpted many of the exquisite shapes that we see in the Tetons today.

Spring comes late to Grand Teton National Park. With an average 16 feet of snowfall, winter holds sway on into April. As snow begins to melt back and open patches of ground appear, the bright blossoms of sagebrush buttercups, the valley's first response to the mid-April sun, begin to appear, heralding spring. Occasionally these flowers will make their appearance in the shadow of a 6-foot snowdrift, but as the spring progresses, they impart a soft golden hue to the sagebrush flats and set a pleasant stage for the elaborate strutting of the sage grouse. Following soon after the sage buttercups are shooting stars. The swept-back rose-purple blossoms of these flowers bob and dip in the warm spring winds. Before green forage is abundant in the valley, shooting stars provide food for elk and deer coming north from their winter ranges. By this time the Uinta ground squirrel has tunneled out through the snow from its winter hibernation and may fall prey to the quick talons of a red-tailed or Swainson's hawk nesting in the nearby pine woods. The small pink and white blooms of springbeauty will follow the melting snowbanks up to 9000 feet in the mountains. Now browsed by deer and elk, their tubers were an early season food for Indians in the valley, as were the roots of the yellow fritillary. The striking golden yellow bloom of the fritillary signals the return of western meadowlarks and the nesting of Canada geese. As the aspens begin to leaf out, the showy yellow arrowleaf balsamroot combines with dense fields of blue lupine to cover slopes and open areas of the valley and to form a colorful fringe along park roads.

The northerly movement of elk from their winter stay on the National Elk Refuge south of the park brings with it the arrival of the trumpeter swans, who share their winter range. Now the northerly waters of Grand Teton and Yellowstone are melting out, and soon the swans, along with geese, ducks, cranes, and herons, will be at work preparing their nests. Like bald eagles and ospreys, swans mate for life and return to the same nesting sites year after year.

By June the sagebrush-grasslands are in full bloom, and nesting activity among Brewer's and vesper sparrows is at its peak. The coyotes eagerly immerse themselves in the business of getting some meat back on their bones, digging up the meadow voles and gophers.

As the summer season comes to the sagebrush floor of Jackson Hole, groves of aspen are alight with the flashing wings of white-crowned sparrows, robins, mountain bluebirds, Swainson's thrushes, red-shafted flickers, and a host of others. The aspen groves of the valley are a particularly rich habitat, harboring countless birds and numerous small mammals such as shrews, voles, and white-footed deermice. Buds and twigs provide food for deer, elk, and moose. The smooth silvery bark of the aspen is a favorite food for beaver, and no aspen growing in the vicinity of a pond or watercourse is exempt from their ambitious designs. Once an aspen is felled by a beaver, the whole family—which may include three generations—goes to work cutting and transporting limbs back to the lodge. The remaining trunk, if too large to move, is soon stripped of its bark.

Gracing the fields and slopes of North America from Newfoundland to the Cascade crest and following the Rocky Mountains south into Mexico, the quaking aspen stands as one of this continent's loveliest trees. The slightest breeze sends the smooth leaves trembling on their slender stalks, and autumn frost sets the leaves ablaze in gold and yellow. In winter, the bare limbs form a delicate lacework among the stands, and the pale silhouette of a single tree burnished with snow seems etched against the winter sky.

The aspen groves of Grand Teton are the result of several factors, including hospitable soils, browsing by elk and moose, and periodic wildfires. Fire effectively clears an area of competing vegetation, and, while killing mature trees, it stimulates the roots of aspens to produce new shoots. Consequently, aspens are one of the first trees to colonize parts of an area after a burn. Eventually, the aspens are replaced by conifers in the orderly succession of the forest. Many of the aspen stands in Jackson Hole are the result of fires that occurred in the middle and late nineteenth century. Fire suppression in this century has reduced the extent of aspen stands in the valley. Recently, however, the park has initiated a natural burn policy that will help restore the function of fire in the ecology of Jackson Hole.

While spring is giving way to summer in the valley, winter is just loosening its grip on the high mountains. With each day the snowline recedes slowly up the slopes of the Tetons, lingering along the avalanche gullies and shaded north slopes and trailing a mist of newly green plant life on the sun-drenched slopes and meadows facing south.

The summer season in the Teton high country is brief and intense. The active phase of the yearly cycle for a number of plants and animals must be fit into a matter of weeks. No wonder that we find the yellow buds of marsh marigolds pushing through a melting snowbank or actually beginning to bloom while still surrounded by the water of an icy snowmelt stream. Fields of yellow glacier lilies spread bright carpets over meadows and slopes, following closely on the heels of the quickly melting snowbanks.

No sooner do the first plants begin to bring the high-country woods

COYOTE.   Coyotes are abundant throughout both Grand Teton and Yellowstone parks, and their calls can be heard most times of the year. They utilize nearly every habitat, feeding primarily on small rodents and some birds and occasionally taking larger animals. The coyotes of Grand Teton are among the largest in the United States and tend to group into packs. Photo by Erwin and Peggy Bauer.

and meadows back to life than a host of mountain-dwelling herbivores, newly awake from their winter slumber, hurriedly forage after the fresh green shoots. Shrill whistles of yellow-bellied marmots ring across the dwindling snowfields, and the small gray-brown shapes of pikas may be seen scooting from the rocky talus slopes where they den to the open meadows where they gather grasses and herbs. While the marmots were hibernating through the winter months, the pikas remained active and often visited the "haystacks" they'd cured and stored the previous summer. Punctuating the mountain stillness with the high-pitched "eek" of their territorial call, these small, round-eared cousins of the rabbit become a familiar sight in the Teton high country.

The full bloom of summer rolls up along the Teton crest in stunning waves of wildflowers. Thin mountain soils receive ample moisture in the form of melting snow. To the west, the Snake River plain acts as a storm conduit. Moisture is carried from the coastal area up into the headwater ranges of the Snake, where it quickly cools and falls in the form of rain and snow. In winter immense amounts of moisture come to the greater Yellowstone area this way in the form of snow. This valuable moisture is retained in the annual snowpack and later becomes available during the hot summer months.

What this moisture means to the high-country meadows, is wildflowers in profusion. In the southern part of the park, north of Rendezvous Mountain, fields of wild geraniums sweeten the mountain breezes, and the delicate blue-white petals of columbines grace the edges of subalpine fir stands. The deep night-sky blue of mountain gentian seems to cool the hot midday meadows.

Farther north along the range, beds of mountain bluebells form a blue-green band of color along the moist draws of hillside meadows. These dense fields of bluebells provide an important food for deer, bear, and elk in their high-country summer range. Elk are particularly fond of these meadows and will often bed down with their calves among deep fields of bluebells.

North of Mount Moran the steep broken topography of the high country gradually gives way to a series of broad open basins and ridges. The deep, moist sedimentary soils of Moose Basin support a verdant garden of subalpine meadow life more suggestive of the coastal ranges than the central Rockies. To hike these basins and high benches is to wade, at times waist deep, through lush fields of aster, arnica, and fleabane. Tall spires of blue larkspur are plentiful, as are the brilliant blooms of scarlet gilia. In late afternoon sunlight, extensive fields of sunflowers—which seem to go on for hundreds of acres—impart a pale golden brilliance to the softly curved meadow slopes, while the cool hue of mountain bluebells traces the distant streambeds and draws.

It is easy to become lost in land like this—lost to all but the essential feeling of fullness and kinship with the wilderness earth. To be alone in a remote basin in the Tetons is to once again come in contact with a place in ourselves that lies deeper than memory—a place that recognizes the unfettered beauty of the natural world as a timeless and ever-present homeland.

Beyond the high meadows and last stands of subalpine trees lies the seemingly barren alpine zone. Even in this stark landscape of snow, cliffs, boulder fields, and ice—where the wind rakes relentlessly across the high passes and talus slopes and the temperature plummets—life has managed to carve a niche. The small succulent plants dwelling among the cliffs, moraines, and scree slopes breathe a singular life and beauty into this harsh world. Perhaps it was the conspicuous beauty of the delicate blue-clustered alpine forget-me-not that led to its being chosen the official flower of Grand Teton National Park. Often found alongside the forget-me-not is the pink-blossomed moss campion. Both these cushionlike plants must send a long taproot into the rocky soil for moisture and nutrients, and their dense, matted foliage creates a warmer microclimate within the plant. This special adaptation helps these plants deal with the severity of the alpine climate. Perhaps the most strikingly beautiful of the alpine flowers is the sky pilot, with its small rounded sky-blue petals and gold-orange stamens. This stunning plant inhabits the glacial moraines around the Middle and South Tetons, lending a note of elegance to the raw, scoured landscape.

Beyond these expressions of hardy delicacy, beyond the spreading phlox, the sparse sedge and grasses, only the crustose lichens feather the rocks, pressing the issue of life further against the extreme edges of climate. Somehow amidst the bluster and thaw of elements, chipmunks and golden-mantled ground squirrels scrape out an existence. But here, as in the valley below, these small creatures disappear into their burrows well before the first winter snows begin to blanket the alpine world.

As fall storms shroud the high peaks, an ancient and instinctual movement takes place among the Teton wildlife. Elk, bear, and marmot, eagles, moose, and Canada geese follow an age-old path of migration or hibernation that will see them through the cold months to come. It is a path from which many individual animals will not return.

The fall migration of animals down from the high country or south along the Snake River valley is one of the great themes of Grand Teton. It presages the coming of winter as well as the dim promise of spring. There are few places left on the earth where the grand drama of seasonal change presents itself so vividly. At Grand Teton National Park, the many elements of that timeless drama still play out their ancient roles, as they have since the world was new.

COLUMBINES, BLUEBELLS, AND DESERT PARSLEY.   To hike the Teton Crest Trail in summer is to sample one of the richest displays of mountain wildflowers any-where. From basin to basin, from one side of a hill to the next, from dry, rocky, south-facing slopes to the cool, moist edge of a northern snowfield, the subalpine meadows are ablaze with vibrant splashes of color, offering new surprises with every turn of the trail.

LODGEPOLE PINE SEEDLING AND MEADOW, OXBOW BEND.   Near the Oxbow Bend of the Snake River, open fields of grasses are punctuated by aspen groves. Along the edges of meadows on higher, drier ground, sagebrush and lodgepole pine are often found. Winter snows can cover this flatland, allowing easy cross-country skiing and snowshoeing access to the Snake River. Bald eagles, trumpeter swans, river otters, coyotes, and moose are common here.

SIDE CHANNEL, SNAKE RIVER. By autumn, the Snake River recedes as the snowpack of the high country is depleted. Its side channels become isolated from the main rivercourse, creating still pools where algae grow. Here the reflection of the sun creates a starburst effect among the smoothed river rocks.

AUTUMN GROUND PATTERNS.   On the forest floor, the soil-building process is
continually occurring. The decay of aspen leaves, pine needles, downed wood,
and other forest debris is accentuated by the visual design of form, texture, and
color. Here we can see beauty in death and understand its vital importance in the
renewal of life.

Designs in nature.   A young lodgepole pine silhouetted against the light trunk of a mature aspen becomes an abstraction, requiring careful inspection to reveal its true identity. We all see the natural world in different ways. At Grand Teton National Park, we have the opportunity to expand and hone our vision and to become more sensitive to phenomena in the natural world.

GRAND AND MIDDLE TETON FROM THE UPPER SOUTH FORK OF CASCADE CANYON
OPPOSITE PAGE: COLORADO BLUE COLUMBINE

THE MOUNTAINS
WHERE LIGHTNING WALKS

The Tetons are a magnificent range, alive with a beauty as fluid and shifting as the water that still shapes their canyons. This beauty speaks when the first roselight of dawn glints dimly off the summit rocks and snowfields, or morning shadows etch and deepen the dark canyon walls; when mist and clouds boil up out of the snowy cirques and basins, or the last shreds of storm cloud trail from the summit like ragged banners in the quiet dusk.

From the valley, soft blue tones gentle the slopes as the rippled skyline gives shape to the afterglow of a sunset. In the high basins, moonlight flooding the granite cliffs and boulders sets the small flecks of mica to glitter, and the alpine landscape becomes alive with a diamondlike sparkle. The distant rocks across a meadow glow with a subtle light that seems almost their own.

And there is the beauty of storms.

The early showers had grown to a serious rain that August morning as I headed from Paintbrush Divide down into the canyon. By the time I passed Holly Lake, the crags were resounding with sharp cracks, and peals of thunder rumbled down through the canyon. The first of the August thunderstorms had come to the Tetons, and my pace out of the high mountains quickened markedly. That evening, after setting up camp in the valley, I remember lingering long past dark, watching as the diffused lightning flashes walked back and forth along the summits of the Teton crest. The distant thunder boomed less menacingly now, and when at last I turned in, I was thankful to be down on the valley floor, a mile below the fury that rumbled softly in the distance.

It wasn't too many hours later that I was jolted awake by a piercing flash of light in the tent and a sharp thunderous clap that seemed to rend the heavens. The downpour that followed—punctuated regularly by lightning flashes and shuddering peals of thunder—fell with the force and intensity of water from a firehose, and it continued for what seemed like hours. After worrying about the river of water that would no doubt be running through my tent, I eventually buried myself in my sleeping bag and managed to snatch another hour or two of fitful sleep before dawn.

In the morning, after the storm had broken, the jagged lines of the steep upper walls of the Grand Teton and Mount Teewinot emerged from their swirling nest of clouds and loomed mistily over the sodden landscape, only to be swallowed up again within minutes. The stormy violence of the night before seemed now an inseparable part of this dramatic mountain landscape. It occurred to me then that in some ways the wild and often unpredictable weather of the Teton Range and the great uplift of the earth's crust that gave the range its birth share a common heritage—the Snake River plain.

After leaving the broad expanse of Jackson Lake and threading its way through Jackson Hole, the Snake River swings west through the cataracts of the Snake River canyon and follows a broad low volcanic plain across Idaho. In winter, the Snake River plain acts as a storm conduit, providing a direct route to the high Rockies for storm systems moving in from the Pacific. As storms rise up over the Teton-Yellowstone high country, moisture-laden air cools, producing the region's dry winter snows. In summer, thermal heating in the Snake River plain forms thunderheads that commonly drift eastward into the Yellowstone and Teton high country, where they cool rapidly and their moisture is virtually wrung out over the high peaks. This creates the afternoon and evening thunderstorms so characteristic of the Tetons in summer.

The Tetons are less than 9 million years old (they're the youngest range in the Rocky Mountain system) and are still rising. Yet exposed along their east flank are some of the oldest known rocks on the continent. The Precambrian gneisses, schists, and granites that make up the breathtaking array of high Teton peaks are part of the very foundation of the continent—commonly referred to as "basement rocks"—and date back about 3 billion years. ("Precambrian" refers to rocks older than the Cambrian period—570 million years before the present.) This makes the rock of much of this young range two-thirds as old as the earth itself.

The precipitous eastern flank of the Tetons is a classic example of a *fault-block* range. That is, the range formed when a block of the earth's outer crust fractured (faulted), uplifted, and tilted. The earth was broken along the north-south fracture on the eastern base of the range. The fault block of the

Tetons is about 40 miles long. As the Tetons began their massive uplift along the Teton Fault zone, the floor of Jackson Hole also began to drop. The same sedimentary rock that caps the 12,605-foot summit of Mount Moran is estimated to be at a depth of nearly 24,000 feet *below* the present-day floor of Jackson Hole. This represents a displacement of about 30,000 feet along this fault system. Since uplift occurred along the eastern part of the Teton fault block, the western slope of the Tetons tilts gradually toward Teton Basin and the valley of the Teton River in Idaho.

As the Tetons began to rise, accompanied by enormous earthquakes, they were assailed by the erosive powers of water, wind, and ice. Because the uplift sloped westward, east-draining streams cut sharply into the rising fault block, deepening the ancestral canyons. As the mountains gained in elevation, they "caught" more weather. Storm fronts—rain, wind, and snow—added further to the erosive forces wearing down the new range.

The mountains easily held the upper hand, however, and by the time the climate tipped toward winter and ushered in the Ice Age, the Tetons had reached a considerable height. The rough shapes of the Tetons were now ready for their final sculpting.

When more snow falls on an area than melts off, it accumulates year after year and eventually compacts into ice. When this ice begins to flow under its own weight, it becomes an active glacier. It was the immense weight of glacial ice, and the quarrying capacity of the rock carried with it, that carved and shaped the Tetons we see today. The serrated ridges and sheer pinnacles of the range are the direct result of glacial carving, as are the broad, deep U-shaped canyons and the jewel-like lakes at their feet.

With the coming of the Ice Age, glaciers from surrounding highlands to the north, east, and southeast flowed into Jackson Hole, and glaciers from the Tetons themselves moved down the canyons to merge with ice on the valley floor. An early advance brought a tongue of ice that reached a thickness of 3000 feet. It and later ice masses melted and left behind a pavement of quartzite cobblestone and gravel over the valley floor.

A final episode of glaciation, begun about 40,000 years ago, further honed and steepened the mountainscape of the Tetons as glaciers advanced down Death, Avalanche, Garnet, Cascade, and Leigh canyons to carve the basins of Phelps, Taggart, Bradley, Jenny, and Leigh lakes. The debris carried and deposited by these glaciers formed terminal moraines, which gave these lakes their present shapes.

Sometime around 12,000 years ago, the climate warmed and the glaciers receded up their mountain canyons and disappeared. Already forest and plant communities were establishing themselves on the moraines and outwash plains, following the warming trend up into the mountains and beginning the age-old process of reestablishing the delicate balance of the mountain ecosystems. The events that have shaped this exciting landscape are not over and have not yet had their final say.

One of the great joys of traveling afoot in the alpine country of the Tetons is seeing this process today. Hiking below the present-day ice of the Teton Glacier or the classically elemental Schoolroom Glacier, one can see the first pioneering lichens and mosses colonizing the raw, exposed moraines. Lower, the alpine plants are followed by sedges and grasses, and where the scant shrubs of subalpine forest have gained a toehold, chipmunks, ground squirrels, and birds can be observed harvesting the ripened seeds.

To visit the alpine glaciers and the thin fabric of life that surrounds them is in some ways to visit the earth's past. Here we witness at once both the creative and the destructive aspects of the earth's natural forces. And here, alone among the stark and windy landscapes, we may begin to understand that the story of earth—and the flourish of life that has made it our home—is one of pressure, turmoil, and opposing forces joined irrevocably to the quieter powers of balance, rest, and the harmonies of water and light.

To fully perceive the beauty of these mountains is to see them whole—their beginnings tucked back in the depths of time, the intricate fabric of living systems they nourish, and the continuing flux of the processes that formed and shaped them and that may one day see them worn down to low hills.

I recall another afternoon in the mountains, high on a shelf above the south fork of Cascade Creek. This time the rains tapered off, and I took advantage of the lull in the weather to hike over a series of rock terraces and broken meadows to a shallow basin. There, a melting snowdrift fed a small stream. As I knelt to fetch water for camp, the quiet murmur of the stream was broken by the sound of scuffing hooves over the rock behind me. Turning, I saw the broad muscular shoulders and unmistakable curled horns of a Rocky Mountain bighorn sheep. His short, smooth blue-gray coat seemed to ripple with movement as he grazed a small patch of meadow grass. Behind him followed two others. From my low position behind a rock, I could see their statuesque forms outlined against the turbulent sky, and they seemed to me to be the embodiment of this high mountain wilderness—creatures as rare and specialized as their rugged and remote environment, yet as stunningly graceful as the mountains themselves. Keeping low, I was able to follow them for some time, until the ram caught sight of the tents at camp and led a hasty retreat down a rocky gully and into some trees. I searched the lower cliffs that evening, but the sheep were long gone, away from me and my trappings of civilization.

Bighorns are scarce in the Tetons, as they are now throughout the Rockies. They are wilderness animals, and as the wilderness shrinks, their numbers also dwindle. But they remain a vital part of the beauty and heritage of these mountains, a final chapter in the long story of the Tetons' creation. Without them—or any of the mountain-dwelling species—the range would be less than it is, its timeless beauty diminished.

AUTUMN LEAF DESIGN . Frost can occur in Grand Teton National Park in almost any month. As summer slides into autumn and the sun swings further south at the equinox, nights become longer and colder. Areas that in the summer receive more direct sunlight during morning hours now harbor shade later into the day, creating conditions for these enchanting frost pockets.

LICHENS AND GRANITE, LAKE SOLITUDE.   One of the more popular back-country lakes in the Tetons, the deep blue jewel of Lake Solitude is nestled in a cirque at the head of the north fork of Cascade Canyon. A moderately strenuous 9-mile trail winds beneath steep mountain walls, eventually arriving at this lake in the heart of the Teton Range. To the east, the summits recede into drifting afternoon clouds.

AVALANCHE CANYON. One of the most remote yet strikingly beautiful areas of the
Teton high country is Avalanche Canyon. Kit Lake and the larger Snowdrift Lake
form the headwaters of Taggart Creek, the main tributary of Taggart Lake. Late
summer snowfields still cling to the slopes, and the summits of Mount Wister
and Veiled Peak seem etched against a summer sky.

DISAPPOINTMENT PEAK AND THE GRAND TETON.   The winter snowpack lingers well into summer in the Teton high country. Above Amphitheater Lake, the rugged peaks still harbor large snowfields in July. The granite, gneiss, and schist that compose these and most other Teton peaks resist erosion. Once part of the bedrock of the North American continent, the Precambrian rocks of the Tetons are thought to be two-thirds as old as the earth itself.

TETON RANGE FROM THE CONTINENTAL DIVIDE. From the alpine reaches of the Teton Wilderness, managed by the Bridger-Teton National Forest, the Teton Range forms the far western horizon. Bordering the southern boundary of Yellowstone National Park, the Teton Wilderness is an integral part of the Greater Yellowstone Ecosystem.

FALLS, SOUTH FORK OF CASCADE CANYON.   In its headwater tributaries, Cascade Creek seems aptly named. Here, the south fork of the creek drops through a narrow notch while Parry primroses cling to narrow banks. The creek hooks around the base of the Grand Teton and, lower in the canyon, slows and ebbs into calm pools. Rippling, it gently glides along before plunging down Hidden Falls and pouring into Jenny Lake.

REFLECTION IN ALPINE LAKE, UPPER PAINTBRUSH CANYON.   The colors of sunset on a jagged spur ridge deepen as they are reflected in an alpine lake. Sunset in the high mountains holds a special charm as the last light lingers on the peaks and the chill of the mountain night settles into the basins and canyons.

SUNRISE, LAKE SOLITUDE.   A fine dew sheaths the alpine world at sunrise. The first rays of sunlight bring it all to life. As the light works its way down the high rock faces of the Teton summits, the still waters of Lake Solitude gather up the muted, gold-tinged image.

TABLE MOUNTAIN IN MORNING LIGHT.   Because of the dramatic rise along the Teton Fault, east-draining streams cut deeply into the lifted fault block, and the highest peaks occur east of the actual watershed divide of the range. Hidden from view of the valley, a series of broad peaks, including Table Mountain, loom over the canyon headwalls. Behind them, the range slopes gradually west to the Teton Basin.

PARRY PRIMROSES. Common to the Rocky Mountain region, the Parry primrose is beautifully conspicuous among its rocky surroundings. Usually found where there is an abundance of moisture, this plant is associated with alpine creeks and shaded niches among boulders. Look for this lovely wild-flower along the high slopes of Alaska Basin and in the upper south fork of Cascade Canyon.

MEADOWLANDS ABOVE MARION LAKE.   At the southern end of Grand Teton National Park, Marion Lake lies in a shallow basin along the Teton crest. Wildflowers embellish this alpine setting during the summer months. Marion Lake is a popular overnight stop for back-country hikers traveling the length of the scenic Teton Crest Trail.

ALPINE GARDEN, ALASKA BASIN.   The wildflower season in the Teton high country is short. During this brief period, resplendent alpine gardens brighten the wilderness landscape. Columbine, Indian paintbrush, and bistort find sufficient soil and moisture to survive in rocks, cracks, and crevices throughout the range.

INDIAN PAINTBRUSH IN MEADOW GRASS. The attention of visitors and photographers tends to be drawn to Grand Teton's magnificent landmarks. Yet the park is a composite of rich detail making up the grand scene. Those who take time to look closely at wilderness patterns will find beauty in nature's simplicity.

MOUNT OWEN AND THE THREE TETONS FROM THE UPPER NORTH FORK OF
CASCADE CANYON.   Along the trail to Paintbrush Divide, the glacier-carved
U-shaped canyon provides a scenic foreground to the Grand Teton . Higher
along the trail, Mica Lake can be seen across the valley to the south. In the lower
canyon, the north and south forks merge to form Cascade Creek.

BRACTED LOUSEWORT, TETON CREST.   The relatively flat tablelands along the Teton crest range from dry rocky scree slopes sparsely populated with low-growing plants to rolling slopes rich with beds of wildflowers. Here, in the southern portion of the park, the candlelike blooms of lousewort, dotted with white bistort, seem to stretch to the far horizon, while the dark shape of Fossil Mountain and the distant pinnacles of the three Tetons dominate the horizon.

GRAND TETON AND MOUNT OWEN.   Each year, thousands of climbers are drawn to the Tetons. The steep, rugged character of the Teton peaks, their general accessibility, and the excellent quality of the rock make this one of the major climbing centers of North America. The range offers a wealth of climbing opportunities, from relatively simple, modest routes to highly technical climbs that challenge the most accomplished alpinist.

GRAND TETON IN MORNING LIGHT.   The eastern escarpment of the Grand Teton
catches the early morning light. At 13,770 feet, it is one of the first peaks to become
illuminated as the sun's rays stretch across the Continental Divide from the east.
Elongated shadows extend to the west of the Teton crest in early morning hours,
giving bold relief to this noble landscape.

MOUNTAIN LAKE AT DUSK.   High above the south fork of Cascade Canyon, dusk brings subtle gradients of color after a summer rain. To the north, the ridges and peaks emerge from soft clouds, and the small glacial lakes reflect the pale colors of a sunset. In the evening stillness the sound of the creek, a thousand feet below, is clearly heard.

SUBALPINE MEADOWLANDS, MOOSE BASIN.   In the northern portion of the park, the deeper sedimentary-derived soils and increased moisture give rise to thick forests of spruce and fir and lush subalpine meadowlands. In Moose Basin, a carpet of sunflowers lends a golden hue to the open slopes. Moose and elk browse here, taking shelter in the clusters of subalpine firs by day.

GRAND TETON AND SURPRISE LAKE.   Surprise Lake, at an elevation of over 9500 feet, is often still frozen in July, as the winter snowpack lingers into summer. The 4.6-mile trail to the lake begins at Lupine Meadow and climbs almost 3000 feet. The hike is well worth it, though—the morning view of the Grand Teton is spectacular.

NEZ PERCE PEAK AND WEATHERED SNAG. The high rocky slopes around the area of Surprise and Amphitheater lakes offer superb views of the surrounding alpine country toward Nez Perce Peak. Remnants of weathered whitebark pine trees add an artistic touch to the rugged landscape.

MOUNT MORAN IN WINTER. Named after the early explorer and artist Thomas Moran, this mountain rises above the clouds to a height of 12,605 feet. When the snow recedes, a great black dike of diabase is visible bisecting the mountain's east face. The dike formed as molten rock welled up into a crack in the older Precambrian gneiss.

FIRST SNOW ON TEEWINOT MOUNTAIN.   As with most mountain ranges, the Tetons create their own weather. Mystical scenes constantly shift as the clouds alternately envelope and disclose the Cathedral group. If you stay in one spot for several hours, you can experience a vast range of moods and tones as the weather patterns change and shift.

SUMMER CLOUDS, SNAKE RIVER
OPPOSITE PAGE: FROST AND PINE NEEDLES

THE VALLEY

IN THE LEE OF THE RANGE

The white head and tail feathers of the bald eagle gleamed in the morning mist. From its perch on a cotton-wood limb above the Snake River, it stared intently into a pool near the bank and seemed unruffled as my raft slipped quietly past. Less than a half-mile down river, I spied two fledgling eagles sharing a large, ungainly nest in the forked limbs of an old cottonwood. Soon one of the adults would return with a fish flapping in its talons, or perhaps a water-fowl—merganser or teal—or a plump ground squirrel. The young eagles had reached such a size that both parents would be kept busy feeding them. Soon they would be leaving their nest and moving on. The mated adults would remain in the Snake River drainage, however, wintering in and around Grand Teton National Park and returning to this same nesting site the following spring. The sight of these majestic birds, soaring on a thermal updraft or poised on a limb over the turbid waters of the Snake, evokes something of the wilderness heart of North America. Their continuing presence here in Grand Teton is a sign that wilderness ecosystems still remain.

There is concern, however, over the future survival of bald eagles in the Rocky Mountain states, where their declining numbers have caused them to be placed on the endangered species list. The ideal habitat along the Snake River corridor in Grand Teton National Park supports many nesting pairs, but even in this protected area their rate of reproduction is barely enough to maintain a stable population. Many of the eagles of Yellowstone National Park to the north also depend on the Snake River corridor south of Jackson Lake and west into Idaho for winter food and habitat. A portion of this river corridor is protected by Grand Teton National Park, but much of it lies outside the park boundary and is subject to subdivision and development.

There are an estimated fifty nesting pairs of bald eagles in the entire Greater Yellowstone Ecosystem. Ecologists use this term to describe an area that includes not only the two national parks and the National Elk Refuge but also the surrounding lands, both public and privately owned, upon which the wildlife populations protected within these parks depend for their survival. Some of these lands include extended winter ranges, nesting and calving habitats, and migratory corridors. In order to ensure that the rich diversity of wildlife populations in our national parks is preserved, close attention must be paid to their needs during those times of the year when they range outside the parks. Management practices in our national forests and wildlife ranges, as well as on adjacent state and privately owned lands, can have serious effects on these wild populations. Wild creatures pay little heed to political boundaries; they function entirely within their ecosystems, any one of which may cross several jurisdictions.

The plight of Grand Teton's bald eagles poignantly illustrates this situation. Of the fifty nesting pairs within the Greater Yellowstone Ecosystem, about twenty nest on lands that are presently unprotected. When these lands are developed, as was the case with at least two other known nesting sites in recent years, the eagles will leave and those nesting sites will be lost.

Although highly visible, bald eagles are not the only birds of prey to make their summer homes along the Snake. Here, too, can be found the osprey. This impressive dark brown and white fish-eating hawk seems to prefer the broken tops of large snags for its nesting sites. Although ospreys migrate south in winter, during the summer they may be glimpsed along the many rivers and lakes of the park, displaying their superb fishing skills. It is always exciting to see an osprey tuck its wings and plunge downward talons-first to snag a trout from the swirling waters.

Osprey young leave the nest by late August, at which time they seem to have completely outgrown their nests. August also finds the beavers along the Snake River hard at work, as evidenced by the many chewed-off stumps that line its banks. Some of these stumps are as large as 20 to 22 inches across. The layers of loess (wind-deposited soils) exposed on some of the river's steep banks are often dotted with swallow holes, and spotted sandpipers bob and scoot along the shore. Soft trills of yellow warblers and willow fly-catchers weave through the stands of cottonwood and blue spruce along the banks, and chipping sparrows frequent the willows. Joining these sounds of summer along the river are the conspicuous splash of a hunting kingfisher breaking the river's surface and the hoarse croak of a great blue heron as it rises noisily from the shallows.

In winter months, the Snake, Gros Ventre, and Buffalo Fork river valleys harbor a sizable moose population. The long legs and wide hooves of the largest members of the North American deer family enable them to move easily through both swamplands and deep snow. Winter populations in Jackson Hole reach high densities in the few areas where willows are readily abundant. Most of the park's moose migrate to summer range in the spruce-fir forests of the high country, but enough remain in the willow thickets along streams in the valley to enable them to be easily observed. Seeing a grand old bull lift its massive head and huge spread of antlers from a stream can be a humbling experience.

When the moose leave their winter habitat along the Gros Ventre and lower Snake rivers, the valley becomes home to a small herd of about a hundred pronghorn antelope that have been wintering on the Green River to the southeast. Unlike the moose, these fastest of the North American mammals are ill-adapted to snow. Deep snow slows them down considerably, subjecting them to predation by coyotes. Consequently, pronghorn must find their winter range on lands outside the valley. Although natural selection has equipped this unique species for successfully eluding predators, it has given them no strategies for dealing with the fences and other kinds of human development that confront them on their winter range.

Pronghorn mate in fall and the young are born in spring. The fawns bed down away from their mothers in tall sagebrush, usually where antelope bitterbrush is also plentiful. Because they have no scent, the fawns are for all practical purposes "invisible" to coyotes, even those that pass close by on their daily rounds.

Perhaps the most misunderstood of America's animals, coyotes have taken the rap for a plethora of crimes, both real and imaginary, committed against domestic and wild animals. Although coyotes are fully protected within the park, there is a year-round open season on them in the rest of Wyoming, and no license is required to hunt them. Nevertheless, these sharp-witted, cunning, and opportunistic predators serve a vital function in the Greater Yellowstone Ecosystem. Burgeoning populations of mice, ground squirrels, and voles would soon eat themselves out of available food if allowed to go unchecked. Other animals that share their habitats would also suffer. Coyotes are one factor in controlling the cyclical fluctuation of these animal populations. Coyotes also serve as the main scavengers of winter-killed elk and deer. Grand Teton is an important habitat for these predators, and the strikingly haunting music of their songs is as much a part of the Rocky Mountain night as starlight.

Though less visible, other predators play an equally vital and necessary role in the delicate balance of the wilderness ecosystem. Mountain lions, lynx, bears, and badgers, as well as several raptorial birds, all maintain breeding populations in the park. These solitary hunters tend to be wary of human presence, and sightings are rare. A large track along a streambed may be as close as most of us will ever come to seeing a mountain lion, but the knowledge that this sleek and powerful creature survives and continues to prey upon the elk and deer populations of the park deepens and enriches our experience of the mountain wilderness.

Throughout the coevolution of predator-prey species, such as the mountain lion and deer, each new adaptive strategy of the prey species necessitates an equal adaptation in the predator species if it is to survive. This in turn creates a pressure for further adaptive strategies on the part of the prey species. Biologists refer to this process as a "spiralling of intelligence," which benefits both species. It is also one of the basic methods by which natural selection functions.

Armed with this perspective, we can see through what may at first appear to be a brutal side of wild nature and recognize the profound beauty inherent in such natural cycles. The few remaining places on our earth where large predator and prey populations still interact are the open doors of evolution, forever refining and honing that elusive element in nature we have come to know as intelligence. It is witness and tribute to our own intelligence that we have had the foresight to preserve some of these populations in the natural environments that sustain them.

❦

Seen from above, Jackson Hole is a mosaic of plant types and biological communities. A green fringe of trees traces the course of the Snake River as it ribbons through the blue-gray plain of sagebrush. Clusters of aspen shiver with each passing breeze, and dense, dark forests of lodgepole pine blanket the lower slopes of the hills.

In years past, the tall, straight trunks of lodgepole pines were used as poles for native peoples' hide-covered tepees or lodges. Lodgepole forests make up one of the most extensive plant communities in the park. The variation within these communities, from the even-aged stands of the younger forests to older mature stands, provides a range of habitats. In summer, elk and mule deer frequent these forests for midday cover. Besides numerous squirrels, gophers, and other small rodents, the forests also provide a home for the cunning and tenacious pine marten. One of the most skilled hunters of the pine forest, this small foxlike member of the weasel family utilizes every bit of its range as it searches for food. In winter, martens tunnel down beneath logs in 6 feet of snow to catch the mice still active at ground level. Summer may find them almost anywhere, as was the case with a certain mar-

BISON. Bison, or buffalo as they are commonly called, are the largest land mammals in the United States. At one time extensive bison herds ranged over much of western North America. Because of overhunting and mindless slaughter, bison verged close to extinction in the late 1800s. Today, about 2,000 animals are protected within Grand Teton and Yellowstone national parks. Photo by Jeff Foott.

ten that frequented my camp on Cascade Creek. One morning I saw him sitting in the upper branches of a cottonwood tree by the stream. Soon, a Steller's jay dropped through the canopy to land on a limb, and the marten leaped for it. Only a last-minute aerial maneuver spared the jay—this time. A few feathers drifting to the ground gave testimony to the closeness of the encounter.

Sharing the trees with pine martens are northern goshawks and great gray owls. The sound of the hunting gray owl's hoot, tracking up and down the pine woods on a frosty autumn night, creates for us yet another mood of these deep unbroken forests.

Dense stands of lodgepole pine spring up after a fire, but the generally rocky soils they occupy make them particularly prone to windfall. Where periodic fire doesn't keep stands in a young condition, older trees become subject to insect infestation. In the 1960s, mountain pine beetles infested many of the pine forests in the park, but this infestation has tapered off dramatically in the past decade. Eventually, lodgepoles may give way to Engelmann spruce and subalpine fir in the forest succession, but this may take hundreds of years. At any point within this period, a fire may recycle the stand back to its beginnings.

Spruce-fir forests are generally found at higher elevations or on cold, wet north-facing slopes. In winter, moose use the lower spruce-fir forests to feed on subalpine fir. Summer months see the passing of elk, mule deer, weasels, and badgers through the shady stands. Clark's nutcrackers rattle the cones at the tops of trees, and mountain chickadees sweep noisily through the lower limbs of the forest.

In the northern canyons of the park, with their greater moisture and deeper soils, Engelmann spruce trees sometimes reach great size and tower over the narrow-coned spires of the subalpine firs. The deep forests of Webb Canyon and parts of Owl Creek and Berry Creek present another world, remote and seldom visited. Glacier-smoothed rock shoulders drop a thousand feet into deep, forested, boulder-strewn canyons. Stately Douglas firs crown the rocky southern slopes and exposed ridges, and monkshood blossoms dot the shade. Quiet, mossy, spring-fed streams break occasionally across the trail. Here as perhaps nowhere else in the park does the feeling of wilderness permeate the air. Afternoon sunlight lingers high along the ridges, and evening may bring a cow moose and her calf to the edge of a willow marsh to feed.

To the south, evening winds are rising in the canyons, and as moonlight breaks against canyon walls, high winds singing through the storm-shaped limbs of the old whitebark pines fill the upper canyons with a special and exciting music. If any of Grand Teton's trees can lay claim to grandeur, it is surely these ancient and elegant pines.

Growing in the scant shelter of the south fork of Cascade Canyon are some of the largest whitebark pines in North America. The graceful spread of their crooked, wind-sculpted crowns is eloquent testimony to both the severity of their mountain world and their strength and tenacity to endure. Lightning, avalanche, fire, wind, and ice have all had a hand in shaping these magnificent trees. It is fitting that they should flourish high in the rugged canyons of this spectacular range.

Summer was leaning heavily toward fall. The first storms had dusted the peaks with snow, and high winds blew incessantly down the canyons from the passes to the west. In the valley, days were still mild, but the evening chill was beginning to have some bite. It was still too early for the fall colors of the aspens to lend their golden light to the fading colors of the valley, but that time was not far off.

I went, one evening, with two friends to the near-peninsula between Leigh Lake and Spaulding Bay to observe a nesting osprey family my friends had been watching throughout the summer. The nest was in a snag over a small marsh in the midst of a large area that had burned three years earlier. Upon entering the burned pine forest, I was immediately struck by the rich greenery of herbs and grasses that grew thickly beneath the charred remains of the forest. Looking closely among the scattered islands of surviving trees, we could see a host of small lodgepole and fir seedlings hidden in the midst of this grassy floor. Here before us were the very beginnings of the cyclical process of forest renewal—a process in which fire had created hundreds of acres of prime elk and deer habitat, not to mention a choice feeding area for a host of woodpeckers and other insect-feeding birds. And then there were the ospreys.

The young had grown to such size that at first we had difficulty distinguishing their cries from those of the adults. The adults wheeled over the nest in great widening arcs but—aware of our presence—refused to land (a tactic protested loudly by the young). Not wanting to disturb their feeding, we watched for only a short while, until the sun dropped behind the range, then turned and started back.

On a blackened spot of scorched earth, beside a charred log, a single pine seedling seemed to glow in the coming dusk. Its bright spreading needles possessed a vigor and energy that seemed remarkable in contrast to the burned earth upon which it grew.

Looking back through the open trees to the shapes of the Tetons darkening against the evening sky, I thought that the small tree had a mission of sorts, a purpose that went beyond its basic struggle for nutrients, moisture, and light—that it was playing a singular and indispensable role in maintaining the diversity and balance of this great wilderness system. It is the combined energy of each single species, living to its fullest capacity, that has created and continues to maintain the harmony we see around us at Grand Teton. We who visit here are asked very little in return for our enjoyment. We are simply asked to understand the wild and elegant balance of the natural world. We are expected to acknowledge ourselves as part of it and to let that knowledge guide each decision as to how we shall live on this earth.

DECOMPOSING LOG, PILGRIM CREEK AREA. It is easy to spend hours in an aspen grove exploring with a camera and close-up lens. The consistent, even lighting of an overcast day allows the rich colors to be recorded. Numerous subjects can be found on the forest floor, from the intricate pattern of veins on a single leaf to a decomposing log playing its role in the soil-building process.

RIVER OTTER. Inhabiting lake shores, streams, and riverbanks, the sleek dark brown river otter may be glimpsed at times slipping into the water. The short legs and webbed feet of this large weasel-like mammal are well adapted for swimming, and it subsists mainly on fish. Photo by Erwin and Peggy Bauer.

MOOSE. The moose is the largest member of the deer family in North America; in Wyoming a mature bull may weigh as much as 900 pounds (Alaskan moose are half again as large). Conspicuous rather than abundant, about 600 moose winter in Jackson Hole and feed on willow and available brush. Summer finds some of these moose in the mountain canyons. Photo by Jackie Gilmore.

ILY PADS AND CLOUD REFLECTION.　Reminiscent of the paintings of famous
French artist Claude Monet, these lily pads seem to be floating on the clouds in-
stead of the water's surface. Such serene settings can be found occasionally along
roadsides and along the short walk to Heron Pond and Swan Lake near Colter Bay.

MOUNT MORAN AND OXBOW BEND OF THE SNAKE RIVER.   At the Oxbow Bend
scenic turnout, Mount Moran reflects in the slow-moving water of the Snake
River. Lodgepole pine, cottonwood, and willows line the banks as the river mean-
ders in a large sweeping arc on its southerly journey through the park. Summer
months bring white pelicans and great blue herons to the Oxbow.

ASPENS, LOZIER HILL.   The interplay of light and shade accentuates the forms of draws and ridges on Lozier Hill. A sense of perspective is created by the pair of aspens sitting on a strong diagonal line. Sagebrush gives the hillside its granular-looking texture.

CATHEDRAL GROUP FROM STRING LAKE.   Narrow, meandering String Lake
connects Leigh Lake with Jenny Lake to the south. Its eastern shore provides one
of the most impressive views of the Cathedral group. The timbered lower slope of
Mount St. John shows evidence of a past beetle infestation of the lodgepole pines.

THE TETONS AND SNAKE RIVER. Schwabacher Landing, along the Snake River, offers an excellent view of the Tetons, particularly at sunrise. Early morning visitors may also be greeted by the sight of moose feeding in the willows and cottonwoods along the river bottom.

TRUMPETER SWAN. Many trumpeter swans winter along the Snake River in Grand Teton, or south in the ice-free waters of the National Elk Refuge. When areas melt free, nesting activity begins, usually in a stand of bullrushes. Cygnets hatch in late June or early July. In three months or so they will be fledged from the nest, and the following spring they will build nests of their own. Photo by Tom Mangelsen.

AUTUMN COTTONWOOD TREES NEAR THE GROS VENTRE RIVER. Cottonwoods are among the most common deciduous trees in Jackson Hole. They usually congregate in the moist lowlands, especially along the Snake River and its tributaries. In winter their naked forms serve as perches for bald eagles. Younger trees are a favorite target for beavers.

SAGEBRUSH AND CATTAILS.   The fragrance of sage fills the air after a thunder-storm. Meadowlarks sing in the distance. This is the open country of Jackson Hole. Moose and pronghorn antelope are commonly found in sagebrush com-munities, along with ravens, sage grouse, and sparrow hawks.

HIDDEN FALLS, CASCADE CREEK. Jenny Lake is fed primarily by Cascade Creek. From both the north and south ends of the lake, trails lead to Hidden Falls, a popular destination for day hikers. A boat shuttle also crosses the lake at regular intervals, transporting visitors to the west shore for the shorter walk to Hidden Falls.

HAREBELLS, EARLY MORNING ALONG OWL CREEK.   The harebell is usually less than a foot tall and bears bell-shaped flowers about an inch long. Found throughout the Jackson Hole area and the Rocky Mountain region, it is especially beautiful when ornamented with frost.

AUTUMN EQUINOX.   By the third week of September, colors are changing rapidly in Jackson Hole. Grasses take on hues of brown and straw, aspens vary from reddish to golden to salmon, and cottonwoods turn a brilliant yellow. When backlit, all these colors are intensified, giving the scene a luminescent quality.

MORNING MIST, STRING LAKE.   A short section of road and a trail follow the eastern shore of String Lake. When the mist lifts in the early morning sunlight, the quiet visitor may catch a glimpse of a moose feeding in willows across the lake. The trail continues back around the west side of the lake below Rockchuck Peak and Mount St. John, passing through meadows and pine forests.

PINE SEEDLING, WEBB CANYON.   The forests of Webb Canyon are among the richest in the park. Spruce, fir, and pine reach impressive stature here, and the floor is thick with wildflowers. In the lower canyon, a rocky bench drops off into Moose Creek, and clusters of lodgepole pine inhabit narrow ledges, terraces, and cracks in the steep rock walls.

LUPINE AND DESERT PARSLEY WEST OF PILGRIM CREEK.   Late spring brings a profusion of wildflowers to the sagebrush flats of Grand Teton. In May and June, dense fields of lupine and desert parsley can be seen along park roads. Other common species observed at this time of year include larkspur, scarlet gilia, and balsamroot. They are preceded earlier in spring by sagebrush buttercup, shooting stars, and yellow fritillary.

BALSAMROOT FLOWERS, SIGNAL MOUNTAIN.   On the south- and east-facing slopes of Signal Mountain, fields of wildflowers flourish in the full sunlight. Views from this promontory include the Teton Range to the west and the Snake River corridor to the northeast. The famous pioneer photographer William Henry Jackson took many black and white photos from Signal Mountain in the late 1800s. Today it remains a favorite photographic spot for park visitors.

ASPEN GROVE NEAR TWO OCEAN LAKE.   In Grand Teton, the aspen groves have been described as "islands of wildlife." Deer, elk, shrews, voles, ruffed grouse, red-shafted flickers, swallows, woodpeckers, chickadees, robins, and thrushes are all commonly found here. Aspen communities are maintained primarily by fire, which stimulates new shoots to grow after a burn.

ASPEN AFTER FIRST SNOW.   Quaking aspens, true poplar trees, are found extensively in the Rocky Mountain region. Their leaves have flat petioles (stems), which cause them to quake or tremble in the wind. This physical characteristic has given rise to their scientific name, *Populus tremuloides.* Frequently reaching a height of 40 to 50 feet and a diameter of 18 to 20 inches, the aspen is one of Grand Teton's most distinctive trees.

ROCKY MOUNTAIN ELK. Elk are among the most visible inhabitants of Jackson Hole. After wintering on the National Elk Refuge, south of Grand Teton, their annual spring migration takes them through the valley to summer ranges in the high country of Grand Teton and Yellowstone national parks and adjacent national forests. The elk of Jackson Hole are a managed population, and hunting is allowed in parts of Grand Teton National Park to keep their populations stable. Photo by Erwin and Peggy Bauer.

EARLY SPRING IN THE VALLEY.   Along the Snake River, small streams and marshes are the first places to melt free of snow. While snow stays deep on the mountains, the sagebrush buttercup announces spring to the lowlands. Soon geese, ducks, cranes, trumpeter swans, great blue herons, and a host of other waterfowl will bring the valley's waterways, lakes, and ponds to life with their feeding and nesting activities.

CROOKED ASPENS IN SNOW.   During their youth, aspen trees are subjected
to the crushing weight of winter snows. The young saplings are bent and con-
torted under the snowpack, and some are permanently deformed into crooked
growth patterns. Tenacity allows them to survive and continue their skyward
surge in groves of sinuous beauty. On sunny days, the smooth gray trunks catch
delicate sidelighting.

WILLOW SWAMP, MORAN JUNCTION. Snow arrives in Jackson Hole early in autumn and remains well into spring. Accumulations in the valley often bury all signs of the sagebrush community and sometimes cover the willow flats. As the weather warms, the melting snow and ice of springtime create still pools, and the willows spring back to form.

LODGEPOLE PINE SNAG.   One of the most common conifers of the northern Rockies, the lodgepole pine has a range extending north into the Yukon and Alaska.   Most of the buck and rail fences in the park are constructed with logs cut from this tree. Individuals that have succumbed to disease or infestation stand as beautiful remnants, especially when graced with a fresh snowfall.

GRAND TETON NATIONAL PARK

Location: Western Wyoming.
Established as national park: 1929.
Size: 485 square miles.
Altitude: 6500 to 13,770 feet.
Climate: Spring—frequent rain, some snow, temperature range from below freezing to 70°F; summer—40–80°F, with afternoon thundershowers; fall—cool and clear, with frosty nights, highs in the 60s; winter—heavy snowfall with temperatures below 0°F.
Accommodations: Lodges, cabins, campgrounds, and RV sites.
Activities: Hiking, backpacking, fishing, boating, float trips, climbing, horseback riding, and cross-country skiing.
For more information write: Superintendent, Grand Teton National Park, Moose, Wyoming 83012.

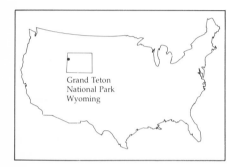

Grand Teton
National Park
Wyoming

GRAND TETON NATURAL HISTORY ASSOCIATION

Grand Teton Natural History Association is a nonprofit organization that operates under authorization of the federal government and with the support of the National Park Service. The association is managed by a board of directors composed of community leaders. Its purpose is to support the interpretive and related visitor-service activities of Grand Teton National Park. Interpretive programs include publishing, purchasing, and distribution of literature about the park, acquiring display materials and equipment for museums and exhibits, and supporting such educational activities as living history demonstrations, environmental programs, and park libraries. Membership in the association is open to the general public.

Woodlands Press
853 Camino Del Mar
Del Mar, California 92014

Distributed to the trade by Kampmann & Company, Inc., New York

Printed in Japan

Pat O'Hara   Tim McNulty

Tina Smith O'Hara

ABOUT THE AUTHORS

Photographer Pat O'Hara bases himself in Port Angeles on Washington's Olympic Peninsula, but his work takes him throughout the West. Pat's interest in photography began while he was a student at Central Washington University and continued to develop while he pursued a master's degree in forest resources at the University of Washington. He has been working as a professional photographer since 1978, and his images have appeared in *Audubon, National Wildlife, Outside, Backpacker,* and *National Geographic,* as well as in Sierra Club and Audubon calendars. His photographs have been featured in the Seattle Mountaineers' book *Washington Wilderness* and in three other large-format books published by Woodlands Press: *Olympic National Park: Where the Mountain Meets the Sea; Mount Rainier National Park: The Realm of the Sleeping Giant;* and *Yosemite National Park: Nature's Masterpiece in Stone.* Pat's equipment for this project included several models of 4"×5" view cameras and a 35mm camera, both with a variety of lenses. He used Ektachrome sheet film and Kodachrome roll film exclusively.

Poet and conservationist Tim McNulty lives in the foothill country of Washington's Olympic Peninsula and has traveled extensively in the mountains of western North America. Since obtaining his degree in literature from the University of Massachusetts in 1971, Tim has published numerous articles on wilderness, wildlife, and forestry issues, and his poems have appeared widely in the United States and Canada. His books of poetry include *Pawtracks,* a collection of Northwest poems, and *Tundra Songs,* a cycle of poems from Alaska. With photographer Pat O'Hara he has co-authored *Olympic National Park: Where the Mountain Meets the Sea* and *Mount Rainer National Park: The Realm of the Sleeping Giant.*

Since 1975, Don and Debra McQuiston of McQuiston & Daughter have been designing and producing exquisite large-format full-color books, elegant smaller guidebooks, and posters dealing with national and state parks and monuments. They have gained wide recognition as

Don McQuiston   Debra McQuiston

Buz Sipes

sensitive and imaginative graphic interpreters of our national heritage. Among the many parks and monuments they have treated are Mount Rainier, Olympic, Yosemite, Bryce Canyon, Capital Reef, Redwoods, Grand Canyon, Cabrillo, LBJ Ranch, and Anza-Borrego Desert. They were also co-authors of *Sandcastles,* published by Doubleday. Don and Debra live and work in Del Mar, California, just north of San Diego.

WOODLANDS PRESS

The purpose of Woodlands Press is to develop and publish works that will celebrate the beauty of America's national heritage and the tireless efforts of those men and women who have labored to preserve it. The Press collaborates with the personnel and associations of the various national parks and monuments, the National Park Service, and outstanding scientific authorities. Founded by Tokyo-based publisher Robert White and the design firm of McQuiston and Daughter, Inc., Woodlands Press is a division of Robert White and Associates, San Francisco, California.

This book was printed and bound by Dai Nippon Printing Co., Tokyo, with manufacturing coordinated by Interprint, San Francisco.
The text paper is acid-free 100-pound Satin Kinfuji Dull.
Typography was by Boyer & Brass, Inc., San Diego, and Thompson Type, San Diego.
The text type is Palatino, designed by Hermann Zapf. The display type is Carlton, designed by Stephenson Blake.

ACKNOWLEDGMENTS

The authors wish to express their gratitude to the staff of Grand Teton National Park, particularly to Sharlene Milligan for her overall guidance, editorial input, and support of this project for the past three years, to Patrick Smith for his many helpful suggestions, to John Daugherty for his historical input, and to Glen Martin for his information on park botany. Bob Wood and Bill Barmore were more than generous with their time and expertise regarding the park's wildlife. Dr. Kenneth Pierce and Dr. David Love of the U.S. Geological Survey provided guidance in clarifying the Tetons' geological origins and offered many helpful suggestions, and Dr. Tim Clark kindly shared his ecological insights. A special thanks goes to the members of the Grand Teton Natural History Association, without whose cooperation and assistance this book would not have been possible. We would also like to thank Jackie Estrada, who edited the book, Florence Fujimoto, who handled the art production, and Eugene Schwartz and Marci Wellens of Woodlands Press for their support. Finally, we wish to thank Leo and Helen Larsen and John Carr for their warm hospitality and excellent mountain company, and Mary Morgan and Tina Smith-O'Hara for their companionship and support both in the mountains and at our respective desks and light tables.

CREDITS

The quote by Osborne Russell on page 7 is taken from *Journal of a Trapper, 1834–1843* by the Oregon Historical Society and is used with permission of the publisher, The University of Nebraska. Photographs other than those by Pat O'Hara have been used with the permission of the following photographers: Page 5—Bald eagle by Tom Mangelsen. Page 7—Porcupine by Jeff Foott. Page 9—Coyote by Erwin and Peggy Bauer. Page 45—Bison by Jeff Foott. Page 48—River otter by Erwin and Peggy Bauer. Page 49—Moose by Jackie Gilmore. Page 55—Trumpeter swan by Tom Mangelsen. Page 67—Rocky Mountain elk by Erwin and Peggy Bauer.

Published by Woodlands Press, a Division of Robert White & Associates.
Photographs copyright © 1985 by Pat O'Hara.
Text copyright © 1985 by Tim McNulty.

ISBN 0-917627-04-0 Softcover Edition
ISBN 0-917627-08-3 Hardcover Edition

Library of Congress Cataloging in Publication Data

O'Hara, Pat, 1947-
   Grand Teton National Park.

   1. Grand Teton National Park (Wyo.)
I. McNulty, Tim. II. Grand Teton Natural History Association. III. Title.
F767.T3038 1985   978.7'55   85-3157
ISBN 0-917627-08-3
ISBN 0-917627-04-0 (pbk.)